There is no greater challenge
or more profound joy
in a woman's life than
that of motherhood.

Library of Congress Catalog Card Number: 98-8698
ISBN: 0-88396-471-6

ACKNOWLEDGMENTS appear on page 48.

 design on book cover is registered in the U.S. Patent and Trademark Office.

Manufactured in the United States of America
Third Printing: August 1999

♻ This book is printed on recycled paper.

### Library of Congress Cataloging-in-Publication Data

The joys and challenges of motherhood : a collection of poems / edited
    by Patricia Wayant.
        p.  cm.
    ISBN 0-88396-471-6 (alk. paper)
    1. Motherhood--Poetry.   2. American poetry--20th century.
3. Mother and child--Poetry.   4. Mothers--Poetry.      I. Wayant,
Patricia, 1953-      .
PS595.M64J69    1999
811'.5080352431--dc21                                    98-8698
                                                          CIP

# The Joys and Challenges of
# Motherhood

### A collection of poems

Edited by
Patricia Wayant

**Blue Mountain Press**®

P.O. Box 4549, Boulder, Colorado 80306

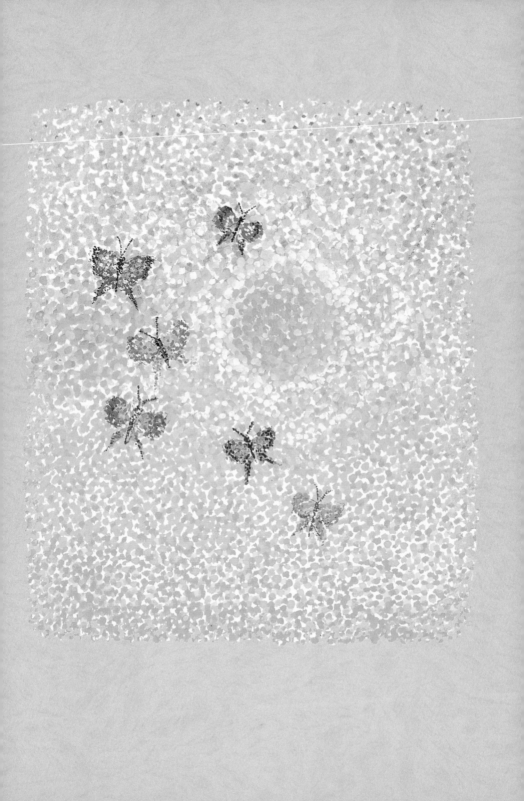

# The Joys and Challenges of Motherhood

A mother is a teacher —
   helping her children to learn about life,
   pointing them in the right direction,
   letting them make their own mistakes
   and then helping them pick up
      the pieces afterwards.
A mother is a friend —
   listening to her children when they need to talk,
   making them talk when they don't know
      they need to,
   supporting them when they are down,
   and helping them to see that things
      aren't all that bad.
A mother is a role model —
   leading her children by her example.
But most of all, a mother
   loves unconditionally
   no matter what her children do or say,
   letting them know that they are not alone
      and never will be,
   for they will always have a home.

— Deborah A. Brideau

# A Lifetime of Happiness Begins When You Become a Mother

Nothing can quite compare
   to the joy of being a mother.
No words can describe
   the happiness
      that having a baby brings
or come close to expressing
   the pride and love you feel
      the moment you first hold
         your child in your arms.
Being a mother is a special gift
   that fills your life
      with happiness, love,
         and a lifetime of memories.

— Deanne Laura Gilbert

# As a Mother...

As a mother, you may
    put yourself second sometimes —
but you will always be first
    in the eyes of your child.
You gave life,
but you will keep on giving
love, support, and wisdom.
No gifts are more priceless
    than these.
Even though being a mother
will never be easy,
remember that it is
the most important job in the world.
Trust your own judgment,
and you will do just fine.
Ask for help when you need it,
take time out for laughter
    and tears,
and trust that experience
will ease some of your fears.
As a mother,
you are shaping the future.

— Jacqueline Schiff

# Becoming a Mother Changes You

Motherhood is an experience
that opens your eyes and your heart
to exactly how magnificent
   and amazing the gift of life is.

When you become a mother,
it is amazing how your feelings,
viewpoints, goals,
and priorities change.
With one look into
your little baby's eyes,
you understand what things
are truly important in this life.

— Donna Newman

Today I woke up
feeling strange
but special
For the first time
in my life
I thought about the fact that I
could produce a baby
Out of me
from he
a little baby
Unbelievable

Sure all my friends
have had babies
but I never thought of myself
as a man's wife
or a child's mother
I am just me, leading
my own life
and in love with he

But today, I pictured
a child building sand castles
and it belonged to us

— Susan Polis Schutz

When you're a new mother,
you wake up just to watch
that tiny person who's so new
and fresh to this world
as they sleep.
You hush everything in the house
just to hear the quiet sound
of their breathing.
You give anything and everything
to protect them.
You are full of hope and joy,
fear and frustration.
Your mind may race with
a thousand questions...
"Will I be good enough?
Can I love enough?
Am I strong enough?"
You are.
You have a lifetime
of learning to share
and a tremendous amount
of love to give.
You'll be great.
All those qualities
that make you a good person
will make you an even better parent.

— Julia Escobar

# Motherhood Is a Life of Commitment and Fulfillment

As a child grows, a mother does, too.

She discovers that motherhood is not the whole of who she is, but it is an integral part. She will never be who she was before her child was born, and she wouldn't want to be.

She learns that love requires not only hugs and smiles, but also firmness and discipline. It means saying "no" and keeping to it, even though a part of her always longs to say "yes."

She learns that this little being who is part of her is also separate from her, as well. A daughter has a will of her own. A son can say "no" as firmly as his mother can — and mean it!

And through the ebb and flow of life, as years pass by, both parent and child draw near and pull away, laugh and cry, remember and dream.

Motherhood is a willing sacrifice, a fulfillment, a never-ending task, and a limitless love.

— Pamela Koehlinger

Your children are not your children.

They are the sons and daughters of Life's longing for itself.

They come through you but not from you,

And though they are with you yet they belong not to you.

You may give them your love but not your thoughts,

For they have their own thoughts.

You may house their bodies but not their souls,

For their souls dwell in the house of tomorrow, which you cannot visit, not even in your dreams.

You may strive to be like them, but seek not to make them like you.

For life goes not backward nor tarries with yesterday.

— Kahlil Gibran

# What Is a Child?

A child is a touch
that bonds you for life
a smile
that makes your heart soar

A child is pride
and hope

A child is someone
whose happiness
becomes yours
and whose pain
is harder to take
than your own

A child is
laughter
that lights up your life
tears
that break your heart

A child is love that goes so deep
it becomes part of your soul

— Barbara Cage

# The New Mother's Motto

"Teach me well, my little one...
To cherish the moments I have with you,
for all too soon
   they will swiftly pass away.

Remind me to pause and touch
   your soft, small cheek,
to marvel at the innocence in your eyes
and the perfect beauty of your face.

Show me how to treasure more the miracle
   that life has given me in you,
to complain less about and praise more
the boundless things you're sure to do.

In the stillness of the night,
when you wake me from my slumber,
help me to realize how truly blessed I am
to be able to hold you next to my breast,
to comfort and cradle you close to my heart.

And as the seasons pass away,
may I never look back in regret
   at what may have been.
May I instead leave a legacy
   for you to follow
as you in turn will one day welcome
   a little one of your own."

— Linda E. Knight

# Some Advice to a New Mother
## (from a Baby's Viewpoint)

"Our first year together
    will be fleeting.
There will be moments
that become memories
to cherish in our minds,
    our hearts,
and our scrapbooks.
We will grasp at images
and hold them for only wisps of time.

I'll change so quickly.
You'll grow as much as I do,
    and in as many ways.
The trying, crying times
    are but moments, too.
They will pass and, in passing,
will make memories that are
as wonderful to hold as I am now.

Trust yourself, for God chose you
    to be my mother,
knowing that you will love me,
    care for me,
        and know me
as no one else ever will."

— Linda Ferree

The love between a mother
and her child
is a bond of the strongest kind.
It is a love of the present,
interwoven with memories
of the past
and dreams of the future.
It is strengthened by overcoming obstacles
and facing fears and challenges together.
It is having pride in each other
and knowing that your love
can withstand anything.
It is sacrifice and tears,
laughter and hugs.
It is understanding, patience,
and believing in each other.
It is wanting only the best
for each other
and wanting to help any time
there is a need.
It is respect, a hug,
and unexpected kindness.
It is making time to be together
and knowing just what to do and say.
It is an unconditional,
forever kind of love.

— Barbara Cage

I can still recall the day my son was born. I can picture his innocent and gorgeous face. I knew in an instant that I would be falling for that face the rest of my life.

He had so much grace about him. As I got to know him and love him, it wasn't long before I knew the beauty that was also deep in his heart.

From a very young age, he was thoughtful and caring. His kindness surfaced over the years on a daily basis. Every day since his birth, I have felt so blessed.

I have learned many lessons from him. He was very forgiving of others and always patient, looking to do things a better way if he couldn't get it done the first time.

His laughter was plentiful and so delightful. Even after a hard day at work, hearing it could make my troubles melt away.

He is a ray of sunshine, and I know the world is a better place because he is in it.

— Betsy Bertram

The first time I held my daughter
was a magical moment.
I remember the first time she smiled;
I still carry that memory with me.
The times I cuddled her
were cradled with tenderness.
Often and silently,
she spoke love to me with her eyes.

I wouldn't trade the countless
fingerprints she left behind
for a dozen unmarked walls.
And all the times her curiosity
led her to my closets and cupboards,
and her imagination left its mark,
only made me love her more.
I loved her giggles then,
and I love them now.

I've seen her in deep thought,
and I've seen her acting silly.
I've captured her moods and our memories
and sewn them into my heart.

When she came along,
I knew she would change my world,
but what I didn't know then
was that I would also gain
a lifelong friend.

— Kathryn Leibovich

Being a mother is wanting
to pick up your children each time
they fall,
but teaching them to
pick up themselves instead.

Being a mother is wanting
to keep your children from all hurt and harm,
but knowing that they must be
taught to take care of themselves.

Being a mother is wanting
to give your children the best of everything,
but knowing they will
value life more if they wait
and work for many of their rewards.

Being a mother is wanting
to love your children with every aspect
   of yourself,
but knowing that some of
   the best love is given
quietly, secretly,
and in ways that they can
understand.

— Karen Kolpien-Bugaj

If anyone ever told
a woman pondering motherhood
how many dishes she would wash,
how many diapers she would change,
or how many spelling words
she would relearn,
she'd probably think twice
before having a child.

If anyone were to mention that the
terrible two's aren't half as
demanding as the turbulent teens,
that school and sports activities
require a mother's lifetime commitment,
and that friends, phones, and malls
are the essence of a young one's desires,
she might have a second thought
or two.

But the funny thing about motherhood
is that once you are a mother,
you can never imagine your life
without the love and joy of your child.
Because with each and every obligation
and the endless amount of responsibility,
there is a wonderful feeling of happiness
that enters your heart
and stays with you wherever you go.

It is the feeling of LOVE...
the most beautiful emotion in life.

— Deanna Beisser

*S*ometimes, looking deep into the eyes of a child, you are conscious of meeting a glance full of wisdom. The child has known nothing yet but love and beauty — all this piled-up world knowledge you have acquired is unguessed at by him. And yet you meet this wonderful look that tells you in a moment more than all the years of experience have seemed to teach.

— Hildegarde Hawthorne

*W*omen know
The way to rear up children (to be just)
They know a simple, merry, tender knack
Of tying sashes, fitting baby-shoes,
And stringing pretty words that make no sense,
And kissing full sense into empty words.

— Elizabeth Barrett Browning

# A Mother's Résumé

I can hear a child's footsteps and determine
   a 102-degree temperature,
While sound asleep and several rooms away.
I can officially score a Little League game
And fit in a carpool pick-up during the Seventh
   Inning Stretch.

I can juggle a nursing baby in one arm,
While cooking a five-course meal with the other.
I can match the correct laundry with the exact
   family member,
Not losing even one sock or shrinking one shirt.

I can read a Dr. Seuss book with one hand,
While winning at jacks with the other.
I can organize 150 women with limited time
   and culinary talent
Into the largest bake sale our school has ever seen.

I can pretend interest in a discussion of taxes
   with my husband,
While planning a PTA fund-raiser in my head.
I can counsel a pre-teenage girl in the throes of
   her first love
Without sounding like my mother.

I can fix a garbage disposal with a broom handle
While saving our cat from a sibling tug-of-war.
I can still fit into the dress I bought for my first job
And truly be thankful that the retro look is deemed
    fashionable.

I can be the perfect smiling hostess and corporate wife
While long-winded clients dissect marketing plans
    and spreadsheets.
I can wallpaper the master bedroom
And watch my son play high-school football
    without screaming or fainting.

Perhaps these talents do not overly impress
Or fit succinctly on a résumé,
But surely they must count as classes passed,
And will help me get a "real-life" job someday.

— Susan Norton

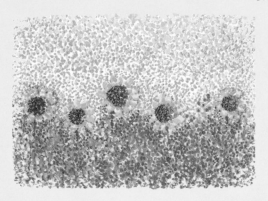

# Raising Children
# Isn't Always Easy

Sometimes it's hard
to be a parent —
especially when you look
at that young person
(the one with the scowl
    and bad attitude)
and you wonder how it
could possibly be your child.
There are times when you
may look at your child and wonder...
Is this the same person who
clutched your finger so tightly
the day they were born,
or who used to look up to you
and think you were
the absolute best?
You wonder when the two of you
grew so far apart,
or where the respect
and friendship
got pushed aside and buried.
You cling to memories
and hold that child
close to your heart,
while you hope and pray
you make it through
one day at a time.
And you will.

Even though it isn't always obvious,
the bond of love never breaks
between a parent and a child.
It gets stretched to the limits,
and it may need constant
mending and repair.
But in the end, you'll both
be proud of its strength
and grateful for its endurance.
Until then, remember that
the only thing harder
than being a parent...
is being a child.

— Barbara Cage

# "The House Didn't Get Cleaned Today"

### A poem to remind you why that's okay

The last time someone asked me what I've been up to, I didn't know what to say ➤ The house didn't get cleaned today ➤ My career didn't advance ➤ My life didn't get any more organized than it was before ➤ My "to-do" list didn't begin to get done; it might have even grown by an inch or two! ➤ I didn't live up to my horoscope's prediction for the day ➤ I didn't even have time to remember which bills needed to be paid ➤ I barely managed to grab a bite of lunch, let alone wonder how to transform macaroni into the "evening entree" ➤ The last time I looked, I don't think my waistline had gotten much smaller, but I'm pretty sure the bank balance has ➤ I'm not driving the latest car, or living in my dream house, or doing lots of other things some people think are essential to do ➤ But I _am_ doing something that's the most important thing in the entire world to me...

I'm cherishing the moments, I'm trying to meet the challenges, and I'm doing my part to raise a very precious family.

— Laurel Atherton

# What It Means
# to Be a Mother

To be a mother is not just
To create life,
But to nurture and shape it.
It is to instill in your child
A sense of absolute security
And self-worth;
To envelop your child
In a protective shield of
Unconditional love.

To be a mother is to have
Within your power to give
An indescribable sense of comfort
That can be found nowhere in the world
But in your eyes, your arms,
And your words.

It is to plant a garden of knowledge
And virtues,
While always weeding out
The external intruders
Of ignorance and prejudice.

It is to be able to look
At your child
At any stage of life
And feel proud of the person
They've become.

— Lynn Barnhart

# Every Child

Every child should know a hill,
And the clean joy of running down its long slope
With the wind in his hair.
He should know a tree —
The comfort of its cool lap of shade,
And the supple strength of its arms
Balancing him between earth and sky
So he is the creature of both.
He should know bits of singing water —
The strange mysteries of its depths,
And the long sweet grasses that border it.
Every child should know some scrap
Of uninterrupted sky, to shout against;
And have one star, dependable and bright,
For wishing on.

— Edna Casler Joll

# Children Create
# the Best Memories

When the years behind you are many
and your hair is white like snow,
the happiest days of your life
will be the ones that echo
with the laughter of children.

Long after your children are grown
    and gone, you will remember...
the pride of counting fingers and toes,
the soft scent of a freshly bathed baby,
those first wobbly steps,
the thrill of their first word,
swinging in the spring sunshine,
dancing in the leaves of autumn,
bundling up for Old Man Winter,
and the magic of Christmas morning
    as seen through the eyes of a child.

Long after the dirty dishes are forgotten,
along with the early morning feedings
    and the dread of chicken pox,
the echo of laughter will remain.
The remnants of hearing a child laugh with glee
will return those special, wondrous,
    child-filled memories —
like that magical, peaceful feeling of love
    you only get when watching
the child you love fast asleep.

— Beth Fagan Quinn

# The Miracle of Life

Life is precious
We hear it so often
it becomes
a litany without meaning
until the moment when
life explodes upon you
Pain and ecstasy at once
place within your arms that perfect
precious entity
The absolute realization of an idea
that words keep in the shadow
of our consciousness
A kind universe
The smiling face of God
Good beyond measure
This tiny individual —
this proof of hope and truth
and all things beautiful
The wonder of creation that is
your child.

— Danielle Morrison–MacNeil

# A Mother's Promise

As a mother, I promise
that I will always try my best
to be a good parent.
I will always believe in my children
and give them the encouragement
they need to achieve their goals
and reach for their dreams.
I promise that I will offer
patience, kindness,
and understanding
when they need it.
I will try to teach them by example
the right beliefs and values.
I will listen even when
I'd rather give them my own opinions.
I will try to be not only
the best mother,
but the best friend I can possibly be.
But most of all, I promise
that I will always love them
without fail and without question.
I will love them enough
to hold them tightly
yet let them go when they need it,
to allow them the freedom
to learn and grow.
I will love them
with all my heart always.

— Deanne Laura Gilbert

# MOTHERHOOD:
## A Celebration of Life

It's LEARNING: You learn from your children as much as they learn from you. As you struggle to help them toward adulthood, they escort you to their wonderful place of innocence, imagination, and delight.

It's HAVING FUN: Get on the floor and play with your kids every day. Create opportunities for fun. Dirty dishes will always be there. Children grow too quickly.

It's LIMITS: Not only do you teach children limits, you learn your own limits for patience and your endurance for long, challenging days. You also learn there is one thing that _is_ limitless: your feeling of love toward your children.

It's WATCHING THEM SLEEP: At the end of each day, you recall the greatest joys and challenges — how they make you so angry and then so happy a moment later. Asleep, though, they are nothing less than angels.

It's TIME FOR YOU: Every mother learns that time for herself is essential to renew and recharge. Two hours alone to yourself when someone else is responsible for your kids can mean days of better parenting. When you feel good about yourself and are happy, everyone's better off.

It's LOVE: Snuggling together for bedtime stories or for popcorn and rented movies. Unsolicited "I love you's." Sloppy kisses and clumsy hugs. Parenting brings more love than we could ever hope for — everlasting, unconditional love of the greatest lengths and depths.

— Donna Gephart

An ideal mother should be
strong and guiding
understanding and giving
An ideal mother should be
honest and forthright
confident and able
An ideal mother should be
relaxed and soft
flexible and tolerant
But most of all
an ideal mother should be a
loving woman
who is always there when needed
and who
by being happy and satisfied
with herself
is able to be happy and loving
with her children

— Susan Polis Schutz

# The Sixteen Gifts
# a Mother Gives Her Children

Hope that is woven into tomorrow ➤ Love that
is sewn into the seam of each new day ➤ Showing,
by being a beautiful example, the path to take to
help you find your way ➤ Warmth and care and
tenderness ➤ Understanding when no one else seems
to comprehend ➤ Believing so much that you believe,
too — that anything broken can mend ➤ Dreams,
hearts, and wishful thoughts are carefully tended
there ➤ No one is better at reflecting life's goodness
➤ A mother is a precious mirror ➤ Within the garden
of her days, children blossom and grow ➤ Thanks
to her encouragement, she always makes sure they
know ➤ The family is a constant treasure, valued
more than any riches are worth...

What a mother gives her children...
are the sweetest gifts on this earth.

— Collin McCarty

# Home Never Feels the Same
# After They're Gone

I wish that I could have
  bottled their giggles
    when they were small
  and collected all of their
    handprints
      from each windowpane.

If I could have done this,
  I would take them out gently
  whenever I need to,
      and spread them across everything.
  Then, I would find such joy
      in remembering.

But I have no giggles
      or handprints
    to hold or to scatter,
  and remembering is somewhat bittersweet,
    for home will never be
    the same without
      the sound of their laughter
  and the gift of their presence
    spilling out from every room.

— Priscilla Wright

# What Is a Son?

A son is a warm spot in your heart and
a smile on your lips.

In the beginning, he is charmingly innocent,
putting his complete trust in you.

He comes to you for a hand to hold and
for the security only your arms can provide.

He shares his tales of adventure and knows
how proud you are of his discoveries and
accomplishments.

All of his problems can be solved by a hug
and a kiss from you, and the bond you
share is so strong it is almost tangible.

Time passes, and your innocent little boy
starts to test his limits. He lets go of your
hand to race into the midst of life without
thinking ahead or looking both ways.

His problems have grown along with him,
and he has learned that you can't always
make his life better or kiss his troubles away.

He spends much of his time away from you, and though you long for the closeness you once shared, he chooses independence and privacy.

Discoveries and accomplishments aren't as easy to come by now, and sometimes he wonders about his worth.

But you know the worth of that young man. He is your past and your future. He is hopes and dreams that have made it through each and every disappointment and failure.

In your heart, your son is precious and treasured. Together, you struggled through the years trying to find the right amount of independence for each new stage of his life, until finally, you had to learn to let him go.

Now you put your trust in him, leaving that son whom you hold so dear totally in his own care. You hope he always remembers that you have a hand for him to hold and arms to provide comfort or support.

Most of all, you hope that he believes in himself as much as you believe in him, and that he knows how much you love him.

— Barbara Cage

# The Love Between a Mother and Daughter

I have worn a locket since the day my daughter was born. Not the kind made of silver or gold; it's made of something much more durable than that.

My locket hangs across my heart and shines more brightly than can be imagined. If you open it up, you'll see pictures of my daughter and me, everlasting and fond memories that began the day she was born. She was so small, looking up at me with eyes so tiny and trusting. I knew from that day forward that it would be my job to ensure that her soul's reflection would always mirror trust.

Before I knew it, she was taking her first steps. Those steps soon took her to school. It filled me with joy to see her smile at me with her front teeth missing, asking endless questions about the world. I tried to answer all her questions so she'd know that they were important.

As she faced each new dawn, I relished every moment that she grew, physically and spiritually, learning new things about life and making new friends who would embrace her in days to come. I also knew that with her determined strength, someday soon she would fly.

It seemed that in the blink of an eye she was all grown up. Her steps were taking her away from the skies she used to play under in the backyard and into a bigger horizon beyond. She was beginning to find her own answers.

I know within the locket, memories will always keep my little girl close to me. The locket sparkles eternally, because it's cast from a love that never fades, the love between a mother and daughter... life's most precious gem.

— Heatherlee Anne Mace

# Children Grow Up
# All Too Quickly

All too quickly,
they grow out of your arms
that held them so close,
and they stand at your side,
holding on to your hand.

All too quickly,
they let go of your hand
and place their arms around
   your shoulders,
hugging you as times go by.

All too quickly,
they are standing tall and strong
   on their own,
independent and self-assured,
letting you see the person they
   have become
and knowing that you couldn't be
   more proud.

All too quickly,
the days of childhood come and go,
but the memories of those times
stay as clear in your mind as ever.
And because they are your children,
they will always be welcomed
   into your arms,
for they will never be too old or too big
to be held close to your heart.

— Deanna Beisser

# A Mother's Love
## Is Forever

There is an overwhelming feeling
of love that fills a mother's heart
whenever she stops and thinks
of what a miracle her children are to her life
and how absolutely wonderful
   her life is because of them.
All parents feel a special
   kind of endless love for their children,
yet there is no way for a child ever
to comprehend the depth of that love
until the day comes
when they are parents, too.

A child is a miracle that never
ceases to be miraculous.
A child is full of beauty
and forever beautiful.
A child is loving and caring
and truly amazing.
Time will pass by,
and so many things will change,
but the absolute joy
that a child brings to life
will only grow deeper
and more important.

— Deanna Beisser